Awakening to God Workbook

AWAKENING
TO GOD
WORKBOOK

A 6-Session Journey to Discovering
His Power and Your Purpose

GERARD LONG
with Bruce Farley

TYNDALE™
MOMENTUM

An Imprint of
Tyndale House Publishers, Inc.

Visit Tyndale online at www.tyndale.com.

Visit Tyndale Momentum online at www.tyndalemomentum.com.

TYNDALE, *Tyndale Momentum,* and the Tyndale Momentum logo are registered trademarks of Tyndale House Publishers, Inc. Tyndale Momentum is an imprint of Tyndale House Publishers, Inc.

Awakening to God Workbook: A 6-Session Journey to Discovering His Power and Your Purpose

Copyright © 2014 by Gerard B. Long. All rights reserved.

Designed by Mark Anthony Lane II

Published in association with the literary agency of Wolgemuth and Associates, Inc., 8600 Crestgate Circle, Orlando, FL 32819.

Unless otherwise indicated, all Scripture quotations are from the Holy Bible, *New International Version,*® *NIV.*® Copyright © 1973, 1978, 1984, 2011 by Biblica, Inc.® Used by permission. All rights reserved worldwide.

Scripture quotations marked NKJV are from the New King James Version,® copyright © 1982 by Thomas Nelson, Inc. Used by permission. All rights reserved.

Scripture quotations marked NLT are taken from the *Holy Bible*, New Living Translation, copyright © 1996, 2004, 2007, 2013 by Tyndale House Foundation. Used by permission of Tyndale House Publishers, Inc., Carol Stream, Illinois 60188. All rights reserved.

ISBN 978-1-4964-0527-2

Printed in the United States of America

20	19	18	17	16	15	14
7	6	5	4	3	2	1

Contents

Preface

THIS WORKBOOK IS INTENDED to enhance your reading of my book *Awakening to God* and to be used as a discussion guide in a small-group setting.

The main priorities for Christ followers are to love God and love other people (Matthew 22:37-39), and to obey Jesus' clear command to go and make disciples (Matthew 28:18-20). The world needs Christ followers who are authentically engaged in loving and reaching people with the good news of Jesus Christ. But in order for us to be equipped to see other people come to faith and maturity in Christ, we must first see these truths go deep in our own hearts and transform us by God's grace.

In addition to your personal study and reflection, this workbook is designed for use in small groups—Christ-centered communities—where wrestling with truth through group discussion and prayer can transform all of us together. Each session is flexible and can be fitted into your church's normal small-group framework, or the workbook can be used as a guide for a new small-group initiative.

As you read *Awakening to God* and use this workbook, please make your personal study, reflection, and growth a priority. That way, you will go to each group session ready to *give* what the Lord has given you and prepared to *receive* what he has for you to receive.

When my work on this study guide was interrupted by an unimaginable family tragedy (shared in the epilogue of *Awakening to God*), my colleague Bruce Farley asked to step in and finish the writing. We felt the message was too important and too timely to run the risk of it not having the greatest possible impact. I'm grateful to Bruce for his efforts and for how he improved the workbook through his wisdom, experience, and insight.

Before you begin this study, take a few moments to read Luke 10:1-6 and ask God to open your eyes to people around you who "promote peace." We'll explore this idea in greater depth in session 5, but I wanted to plant a seed, right at the outset, as you prepare to be *awakened to God* and become a worker sent out into the "harvest field."

Foreword

As PASTOR BILL HYBELS has memorably said, the local church is the hope of the world. *Awakening to God* was written to help the local church bring transformation to our society. The early church "turned the world upside down"[1] when they were equipped by the Holy Spirit and obeyed the teaching of Jesus Christ to follow him and "fish for people."[2] *Awakening to God* is based on the same principles of equipping and teaching.

God has called you, as a follower of Jesus Christ, to know him and participate with him in his rescue plan for the men and women of the world—including your family, neighbors, friends, and coworkers. God's plan for you has been in place since before the creation of the universe, and he has uniquely equipped you with gifts, abilities, and experiences that enable you to carry out the plan. When you find the "sweet spot" of God's calling and purpose for your life, you will find contentment, fulfillment, and great joy there as well.

As you study *Awakening to God* on your own and then participate in the small-group discussions, listen carefully to what God says to you. Recognize what he has placed in your hands, and be courageous in making commitments to use your gifts and abilities to draw others to Christ.

This workbook is designed to help you in three particular ways:

1. To help you grow in your personal relationship with Jesus Christ (because everything flows from your relationship with him). In particular, we want to help you grow in your knowledge of Scripture and your understanding and awareness of the Holy Spirit in your life.

2. To help you realize and understand how special you are to God. He has a unique plan to "send you out to fish for people."[3] And he has promised to equip you with everything you need to complete his plan for you. God wants you to participate with him in his purposes; to live only to please him; and to complete his will for your life.

3. To help you know and understand that you are part of God's amazing work and purpose on earth. We are all designed to fulfill God's plan as part of the body of Christ, the church. Our prayer is that you would be supported and encouraged by other Christ followers and have at least one other Christ follower with whom you can walk closely as you "fish for people" and "turn the world upside down."

How to Use This Study

JESUS SAID, "IF YOU HOLD to my teaching, you are really my disciples. Then you will know the truth, and the truth will set you free."[4] What you are about to experience in your small group is an opportunity to have a new *awakening* in your walk with Jesus. I pray it will guide you into greater truth and freedom, and will also lead you to a change in lifestyle, one that will align your life with the life of Christ. I pray that the rest of your time on earth will be dedicated to reaching and connecting with people who are spiritually sinking—that is, people who are without Christ and without hope. God wants to use you to be his hands and feet in his great rescue plan for the world.

Each week of the study is divided into five sections: Engage, Prepare, Discuss, Apply, and Further Reading. *Engage* is designed to connect you to the book *Awakening to God: Discovering His Power and Your Purpose* and to give you some foundational principles that apply to the chapter reading for each week. *Prepare* is your opportunity to answer the questions on your own before the group discussion. This time of personal preparation is vital to your own growth and to the success of your small group. *Discuss* is the main group time, when you and other group members can share with one another the answers you've written during your preparation time. *Apply* will help you put into practical action the principles you've learned.[5] Each session ends with *Further Reading*—a list of verses to take you deeper into God's Word.

ENGAGE

Before each group meeting, engage with the week's topic by reading the relevant chapters in *Awakening to God*. Ask God to speak to you as you read, and listen to what he says to you. Remember, whatever God asks you to do, he will provide you with the grace to carry it through. He is looking for your *availability* to participate with him in reaching people who are spiritually sinking.

As further preparation for each small-group session, review the list of principles that apply to each week's study. Also, to fully immerse yourself in the topic, read and meditate on the Further Reading for each session.

PREPARE

Awakening to God is thoroughly grounded in Scripture, and what you will discuss in your small group is what Jesus taught his disciples. We should always allow God's Word to speak to us, and this means having a heart of humility. We don't have all the answers; we're dependent on the Holy Spirit to guide us "into all the truth."[6] Meditate on the key Scriptures for each small-group session—and, if you can, memorize all or part of them.

DISCUSS

Jesus taught his disciples in a group setting, and his teaching method was question based (for example, "Who do you say I am?"[7]). If you think about it, we actually learn more deeply when we have to wrestle with questions rather than try to absorb a list of facts. Think deeply about the questions and your personal and group answers, and make them your own. For this process to really be effective, you must be totally honest and fully engaged. Remember, your contribution may help others in the group to understand what God is saying to them.

Many of the questions in this workbook are drawn from specific passages in *Awakening to God*. We encourage you, if time allows during your small-group meetings, to read these passages aloud as a group before answering the questions. Experience has shown that reading aloud together enhances discussion and encourages greater participation.

This should be a *group* experience. No one person should dominate; instead, everyone should feel accepted, valued, and free—*encouraged*—to contribute. In this way, God will speak powerfully through the group dynamic.

We are created for God's pleasure. The best way we can please and glorify him is by completing the work he has prepared for us to do.[8] Spend some time in each small-group session worshiping God from your heart—in song, in spoken communication, in silence, in prayer, and in loving and blessing one another.

APPLY

Because of our human weakness and our busy lives, we often forget to put the Word into action, even after God has spoken to us. As a result, we see little or no change in our lives. As part of session 1, identify (and agree with) one or two others in the group and commit yourselves to pray and hold one another accountable to carry out the application items from each small-group session. It is only when you "continue to follow [Jesus]" and "let your roots grow down into him, and let your [life] be built on him" that "your faith will grow strong in the truth"[9] and you will be equipped to share the good news of Jesus Christ with the people around you who are sinking.

WHAT YOU'LL NEED

Before your first meeting, be sure that each group member has a copy of the following three books:

- *Awakening to God: Discovering His Power and Your Purpose* by Gerard Long
- *Awakening to God Workbook*
- a Bible

AWAKENING TO GOD'S LOVE AND PURPOSE

ENGAGE

Read chapter 1 in *Awakening to God: Discovering His Power and Your Purpose.*

If you have surrendered all of your life to Christ (at least as far as you know), you don't need to fret about whether you're in the sweet spot of his will for you. Instead, keep your focus on Jesus and on loving him more (Psalm 37:4). He will guide you with his love and give you peace through the Holy Spirit (Isaiah 30:21). Scripture teaches that suffering for the Kingdom of God—which is different from suffering for our own bad decisions—is a high calling (Genesis 50:20; Philippians 1:29, 3:8). Ultimately, God's perfect plan is that we will come to know Christ more and more.

Principles for obeying God's will for your life

- Love God and people (Matthew 22:37-40)

- Go and make disciples for Jesus Christ (Matthew 28:19-20)
- Guard your heart (Proverbs 4:23)
- Make time with God your first priority (Matthew 6:33)
- Walk by faith (2 Corinthians 5:7)
- Do everything for God's glory (Isaiah 43:21, 61:1-3)
- Do everything with all your heart, as working for the Lord (Ecclesiastes 9:10; Colossians 3:23-24)
- Be a good steward of all that God has given you (Luke 12:48, 19:11-27)

PREPARE

Why have you decided to read the book *Awakening to God*? What do you hope to gain from your time of studying the book on your own and discussing it with others in a small group? Write your initial thoughts here:

Awakening to God's Purpose

"For I know the plans I have for you," declares the LORD, "plans to prosper you and not to harm you, plans to give you hope and a future." (Jeremiah 29:11)

[Before discussing the following question during your small-group time, have someone read aloud the paragraph on page 1 in *Awakening to God* that begins "I still remember . . ." and ends ". . . *life made out of perfect love.*"]

1. At the beginning of chapter 1 in *Awakening to God*, Gerard Long tells the story of Valentine's Day 1980, the day he first truly awakened to God. Have you had a similar awakening in your own life? What do you remember about the day when you first believed in Jesus and surrendered your life to his lordship? Write down your thoughts and feelings about that time in your life:

2. How have you dealt with hard times in your life?
   How did God use that time to awaken you to his
   love and purpose for you?

Awakening to God's Lordship

*You will seek me and find me when you seek me with all your
heart.* (Jeremiah 29:13)

*Therefore, I urge you, brothers and sisters, in view of God's mercy,
to offer your bodies as a living sacrifice, holy and pleasing to
God—this is your true and proper worship. Do not conform to the
pattern of this world, but be transformed by the renewing of your
mind. Then you will be able to test and approve what God's will
is—his good, pleasing and perfect will.* (Romans 12:1-2)

[Before discussing the following question during your small-group time, have
someone read aloud the paragraph on page 7 in *Awakening to God* that begins
"I encourage you to consider . . ." and ends ". . . into a full and satisfying life."]

3. In your day-to-day life, what does it look like for
   you to be someone who seeks the Lord with all your
   heart and offers your body as a "living sacrifice" to

God? As you answer these questions and share your thoughts with the group, be real and practical—not theoretical or idealistic.

Awakening to God's Love

I pray that you, being rooted and established in love, may have power, together with all the Lord's holy people, to grasp how wide and long and high and deep is the love of Christ, and to know this love that surpasses knowledge—that you may be filled to the measure of all the fullness of God. (Ephesians 3:17-19)

[Before discussing the following question during your small-group time, have group members read aloud the passage on pages 9–10 in *Awakening to God* that begins "Four things immediately . . ." and ends ". . . I was now enjoying."]

4. Gerard says that four things immediately changed in his life when he fully surrendered himself to Christ: he was head over heels in love with Jesus; he had a newfound love for God's Word; he desired to live a holy life (first seen when he stopped swearing); and he developed a deep love and concern for other

people. Which of these changes resonates the most with you at this point in your walk with God? Why? Be ready to share your answer with the group.

5. How does an awareness of God's love for you increase your heart of love for others and your desire to tell them about Jesus?

DISCUSS

As you begin your first group time together, take a moment to pray for God's purposes to be accomplished as you study and grow together. Then go through the questions together, reading aloud where indicated, and share your answers with the group.

APPLY

Based on your reading of chapter 1 in *Awakening to God* and this week's group discussion, write down for yourself—and feel free to share with the group—practical areas in which you can grow.

As you think about God's love for you—and his desire to express Christ's love *through* you—take a moment to write down the names of at least five people you know who don't know Christ. Commit yourself to start (or continue) praying for these people and engaging with them in a more intentional way. Write their names here:

Connect with one or two other people in the group and team up to pray together weekly for the areas of growth you've identified and the people God has prompted you to pray for and engage with.

FURTHER READING

Job 23:10; Psalm 23; Psalm 127:1; Zechariah 4:6; Matthew 21:1-3; John 3:8; John 3:27; John 4:34; John 5:30; John 6:38; John 8:29; Acts 9:11-12, 15-16; Acts 13:2; Philippians 2:13; 2 Thessalonians 1:11; Hebrews 1:3

AWAKENING TO THE HOLY SPIRIT: POWER FOR LIVING

ENGAGE

Read chapter 2 in *Awakening to God: Discovering His Power and Your Purpose.*

Scripture teaches that God fills the hungry with good things and satisfies the thirsty (Matthew 5:6; Luke 1:53; John 7:37-39). His love, gifts, and presence come to us through the Holy Spirit. Our responsibility is to keep our hearts hungry for God and open to receiving more of him in our lives (Proverbs 4:23).

Principles for keeping your heart hungry and open for more of God in your life

- Nurture and develop your love for God. Set aside regular time with him, meditate on his Word, listen to worship music, consider God's beauty in the person of Jesus and in creation.

- Regularly ask the Holy Spirit to search your heart for anything that grieves God (Psalm 139:7-10, 23-24).
- Develop a growing relationship with the Holy Spirit and an increased sensitivity to his work and presence. Your body is a temple of the Holy Spirit (1 Corinthians 6:19-20; 2 Corinthians 6:16). He sees and hears everything you do and wants to help, guide, and equip you to live an abundant life in Christ.
- Ask the Lord to make you hungry to know him more. Ask him to help you trust and surrender every part of your life to him, and to be open to everything he wants to do *in* you and *through* you. Trust that God's grace is sufficient and will equip you with everything you need to do his will.

PREPARE

1. In one sentence, how would you describe the role and the importance of the Holy Spirit in your life over the last month?

Why do we need to be refilled?

Do not get drunk on wine, which leads to debauchery. Instead, be filled with the Spirit. (Ephesians 5:18)

[Before discussing the following question during your small-group time, have group members read aloud the passage on pages 17–18 in *Awakening to God* that begins "I want to be clear . . ." and ends ". . . God's grace enables us to do this."]

2. When you look at your walk with God and then read that there are "many ways to 'spring a leak' and begin to lose your sense of the Holy Spirit's filling in your life,"[10] what areas of your life come to mind? Be ready to share these with the group. Hearing the challenges we all face helps us to know that we're not alone in our efforts to live a Spirit-empowered life.

How to become more like Jesus

Hope does not put us to shame, because God's love has been poured out into our hearts through the Holy Spirit, who has been given to us. (Romans 5:5)

The fruit of the Spirit is love, joy, peace, forbearance, kindness, goodness, faithfulness, gentleness and self-control. Against such things there is no law. (Galatians 5:22-23)

[Before discussing the following question during your small-group time, have group members read aloud the passage on page 19 in *Awakening to God* that begins "When we are in fellowship . . ." and ends ". . . keep my heart aligned with God's will."]

3. What is your response to Gerard's assertion that the more we surrender our will to the Holy Spirit, the more Jesus is revealed *to* us and *through* us, and the more the Kingdom of God will reign in our lives? In what ways have you experienced this same truth in your own life?

4. Describe a time when you sensed God pour his love into your heart by the Holy Spirit.

The filling of the Holy Spirit

You will receive power when the Holy Spirit comes on you; and you will be my witnesses in Jerusalem, and in all Judea and Samaria, and to the ends of the earth. (Acts 1:8)

[Before discussing the following question during your small-group time, have group members read aloud the passage on page 20 in *Awakening to God* that begins "Because I know firsthand . . ." and ends ". . . live abundantly that day."]

5. What's your response to Gerard's description of the ongoing filling of the Holy Spirit? How does it encourage you or challenge you? How can you experience more of the Holy Spirit in your life?

6. Are you hungry for more of God in your life? Do you really want to know him more? What would that look like in your life?

7. Are you open to everything God has for you? What, if anything, is holding you back from regularly asking God to fill you with the Holy Spirit?

DISCUSS

As you begin your group time together, take a moment to pray for God's purposes to be accomplished as you study and grow together. Share your answers to the above questions with the rest of the group. As you share your experiences and hear what others share, be open to new ways in which God may want you to experience more of him.

APPLY

Learning to live a Spirit-filled life—a life of living in power and loving the people Jesus came "to seek and to save"—is at the core of what it means to be a Christ follower.

Take some time to reflect and write down how God spoke to you through this chapter—specifically, which spiritual disciplines (reading God's Word, praying, listening for and obeying his voice) he is calling you to go deeper in.

As your group meeting comes to a close, get together with one or two other group members to pray for the people whose names you wrote down at the end of session 1. Ask God to fill each of you with the Holy Spirit—to give you the power to love and the power to live with the courage, compassion, and humility of Jesus. Ask the Holy Spirit to move in greater ways to draw the people you're praying for to Jesus. Ask him to guide you into constructive engagement with them. At the end of your personal study—and again as a group at the end of your meeting time—pray the following prayer out loud:

> *Lord, make me hungry to know you more and to surrender every part of my life to you. Please help me to be open to everything you want to do in me and with me. I want to trust that your grace is sufficient for me and will equip me with everything I need to do your will. Amen.*

FURTHER READING

John 14:16-18, 26-27; John 16:7-14; Luke 11:9-13; Acts 1:4-5; 1 Corinthians 12:7-11; 2 Corinthians 13:14; Galatians 5:22-23; Ephesians 3:14-21; Philippians 2:1-2; Philippians 3:8-11

AWAKENING TO OUR CALLING: GO AND MAKE DISCIPLES

ENGAGE

Read chapter 3 in *Awakening to God: Discovering His Power and Your Purpose.*

As Scripture teaches, without a vision people perish or go astray (Proverbs 29:18). God wants us to share his love and concern for the lost and to have "eyes and ears" for the people in our lives that he wants us to befriend and witness to. The greatest challenge will be to change our lifestyle to make room to be more intentional in building relationships and making friends with people who don't know Christ.

Principles for obeying Jesus' command to "go and make disciples"

- Be filled with the Holy Spirit (Ephesians 5:18). Consider the experience of the first disciples before and after Pentecost, and ask God to pour his love and power into your heart by the Holy Spirit (Acts 1:8; Romans 5:5).

- The first disciples turned the world upside down by following Jesus' command to *go*. Be courageous—go for it. The Kingdom of God is *motion activated*. As soon as we break camp to win precious souls for Christ, we enter into a cosmic battle. There will be opposition. Stop the excuses and step out in faith.

- Meditate on Revelation 12:11. What will you sacrifice to see your family, friends, neighbors, and nation won for Jesus?

PREPARE

Immediately prior to his ascension to heaven, Jesus left us with simple marching orders: "Go and make disciples." In other words, live with the clear priority of loving people and befriending them, with the hope of seeing them come to faith and maturity in Jesus Christ.

When you consider that going and making disciples for Jesus is what should define our lives as Christ followers, what's your honest response? In what ways does it challenge you, scare you, give you joy? How can you make discipleship a priority in your life?

Awakening to our calling

Therefore go and make disciples of all nations, baptizing them in the name of the Father and of the Son and of the Holy

Spirit, and teaching them to obey everything I have commanded you. And surely I am with you always, to the very end of the age. (Matthew 28:19-20)

1. Knowing that God's grace is everpresent to help you change and grow, how are you living out Jesus' clear command from Matthew 28:19-20 in your life?

[Before discussing the following question during your small-group time, have group members read aloud the passage on pages 27–28 in *Awakening to God* that begins "How does Jesus want . . ." and ends ". . . equips us and sustains us."]

2. When you read the list of things that Jesus did on earth (page 27 of *Awakening to God*), what stands out to you—and why?

Awakening to eternal destiny

3. What is your initial response to the idea of hell—
   especially to the quote from C. S. Lewis (pages
   29–30 of *Awakening to God*)? How does the reality
   of hell motivate you to share the gospel?

Going with God's power and presence

[Before discussing the following question during your small-group time, have
group members read aloud the passage on pages 31–32 in *Awakening to God*
that begins "The best way we can prepare . . ." and ends ". . . prove to be my
disciples."]

4. How does the simple act of "abiding" in Christ
   (obeying his Word and living in the power of the
   Holy Spirit) empower you to fulfill your calling to
   see people come to know Christ and grow in him?

5. Gerard tells the stories of his move from London to New York City and how God used the Chinese student Lin to bring Lin's mother in China to Christ. Your stories may not be as dramatic, but how is God leading and working in your life as you're reading and applying this book?

Since, then, you have been raised with Christ, set your hearts on things above, where Christ is, seated at the right hand of God. Set your minds on things above, not on earthly things.
(Colossians 3:1-2)

[Before discussing the following question during your small-group time, have group members read aloud the passage on pages 38–39 in *Awakening to God* that begins "At an Alpha event . . ." and ends ". . . life on this earth."]

6. When you read the story of Nick Vujicic in light of Colossians 3:1-2, what does it make you think and feel? In what ways are you setting your heart on things above?

7. Clearly, we live in a dark time. How does it make you feel to realize that—because of Christ in you— you are called and privileged to be "the light of the world" (Matthew 5:14-16)?

8. In what areas of your life can you be more intentional to build relationships and make friends with people who don't know Christ? Answer this question during your personal preparation time, and be ready to suggest practical application steps in your discussion with your accountability partners in the group.

DISCUSS

As you share your answers to the above questions, pay attention to how God is awakening your heart to go and make disciples.

APPLY

Based on your answer to question 8 above, think of an activity—such as going out for coffee or a meal, shooting some hoops, going for a hike (whatever fits your lifestyle and the lifestyle of your friend)—that you can do with one (or more) of the people you're reaching out to. Pray for God's guidance; then make the connection and put your plan into action. Agree with your group partners to hold one another accountable to pray for and reach out to the people on your list— especially those whom God is specifically leading you to at this time.

FURTHER READING

Matthew 5:13-16; Matthew 6:19-21; Matthew 25:41, 46; Luke 12:48; John 5:28-29; John 17:15; Acts 1:8; Acts 4:20; Acts 17:6-7; Acts 20:24; Romans 10:14-15; 2 Corinthians 4:16-18; 2 Corinthians 5:10, 20; 2 Thessalonians 1:3-10

AWAKENING TO BROKENNESS AND ETERNITY

ENGAGE

Read chapters 4 and 5 in *Awakening to God: Discovering His Power and Your Purpose.*

When we experience suffering and tragedy, those are times when we often find ourselves questioning God. Yet, even in the midst of our questioning, we may also grow closer to God. Think of some of the hardest times you've walked through in your life. In what ways were they hard, and in what ways did God meet you there?

Principles for living "awakened" to eternity

- There's something about adversity that purifies our motives, deepens our passion for souls, and opens our eyes to the promise of eternity.
- Rewards are mentioned more than one hundred times in the New Testament—not to bribe us, but to encourage us. Setting our hearts and minds on our eternal reward frees us to live according to God's will here on earth.
- Having a godly view of eternity sets us free to give ourselves fully to God's will for our lives. "Teach us to number our days, that we may gain a heart of wisdom" (Psalm 90:12).
- Only by being filled afresh with the Holy Spirit can we truly have God's heart for the lost, the sinking, the battered, and the bruised. Ask God to give you the power to witness for him, to be courageous enough to change your lifestyle so that you intentionally make friends with people who don't know the Lord. Ask God to open your eyes to eternity and to help you make wise decisions about how you live your life on earth.

PREPARE

Awakening through brokenness

*For our light and momentary troubles are achieving for us an
eternal glory that far outweighs them all. So we fix our eyes not on*

what is seen, but on what is unseen, since what is seen is temporary,
but what is unseen is eternal. (2 Corinthians 4:17-18)

[Before discussing the following question during your small-group time, have group members read aloud the passage on pages 46–51 in *Awakening to God* that begins "There's something about affliction . . ." and ends ". . . a deep appreciation for eternity had now been released."]

1. When you read Gerard's story about the death of his son Alex—written by a man who was and is serving God with all his heart—what does it make you think, and how does it make you feel?

2. In what ways can the difficulties of life help us see God's goodness more clearly—even in the midst of the pain? In what ways do those difficulties open our eyes and motivate us to see as many people won to Christ as possible?

Awakening to eternity

Teach us to number our days, that we may gain a heart of wisdom.
(Psalm 90:12)

[Before discussing the following question during your small-group time, have group members read aloud the paragraph on page 60 in *Awakening to God* that begins "The quality of your decisions . . ." and ends ". . . about how we live today."]

3. In what ways does being heavenly minded help us to number our days? How does it help us to make the most of our impact on others for eternity?

4. Review the accounts of the lives of Jim Elliot, Jonathan Edwards, and C. T. Studd at the end of chapter 5 of *Awakening to God*. In what ways is God speaking to you through these stories?

5. To what degree does the call we all have to see others come to know Christ feel *urgent* to you? In what ways might God be wanting to change how you feel?

DISCUSS

Begin your discussion by having some of the group members share their experiences of growing closer to God through suffering and tragedy. As others share, be sure to listen *gently*, and don't try to "interpret" what God might have been doing through those difficult circumstances.

APPLY

Both alone (during your preparation time) and with one or two other people in the group, take time to reflect on and pray about the pain you've experienced in your life. Consider how God can use that pain to minister to others through you. What opportunities is he opening for you right now?

FURTHER READING

Genesis 50:20; John 12:24-26; John 14:26; 1 Corinthians 10:13; 2 Corinthians 1:3-7; 2 Corinthians 2:14; Hebrews 2:17-18; Hebrews 4:15-16; Hebrews 5:2, 7-9

AWAKENING TO OUR OPPORTUNITY AND GOD'S PROVISION

ENGAGE

Read chapters 6 and 7 in *Awakening to God: Discovering His Power and Your Purpose.*

Scripture teaches that God has equipped every individual with specific gifts, abilities, and experiences (even brokenness) that he wants us to use to complete the work he has planned for us since the creation of the universe (Ephesians 2:10). Believe that God has planted you in your family, neighborhood, and workplace and that he wants you to be his hands, feet, and mouthpiece to show people his love. Commit to live an intentional lifestyle of reaching out to those who don't know Christ, through prayer and by developing genuine, trusting relationships. Don't let discouragement take root in your heart.

Principles for having a bigger vision for God's calling on your life

- *Belief.* Increase your vision of God and how he is working in you to enable you to participate in his eternal plan and purpose (John 6:29; Romans 11:36–12:2; Philippians 2:13).
- *Grace.* Know that God's grace will equip you with everything you need to do his will (Hebrews 13:20-21). Every gift, ability, and experience you have has been given to you by God for his glory (1 Corinthians 8:6).
- *Stewardship.* God wants us to be faithful stewards, to use the gifts he's given us to fish for people and to extend God's Kingdom on earth. You are where you are, not to do your own will, but to do the will of God (John 5:30; John 6:38; John 8:29).
- *Prayer.* Prayer is the most powerful tool God has given us to extend his Kingdom and to fish for people.

> *Lord, thank you for your grace, which equips me with everything I need to complete the work you have prepared for me to do. I choose to believe that you have planted me in my family, neighborhood, and workplace to be your witness and to fish for people who are sinking. I commit to live a lifestyle of reaching out and befriending people who don't know Christ. Amen.*

PREPARE

1. Is it the privilege and responsibility of every
   Christian to "fish" for people—living our lives
   intentionally and building relationships that we hope
   will lead people to know and follow Jesus Christ?
   Why or why not?

Awakening to our opportunity

*As Jesus was walking beside the Sea of Galilee, he saw two brothers,
Simon called Peter and his brother Andrew. They were casting a
net into the lake, for they were fishermen. "Come, follow me," Jesus
said, "and I will send you out to fish for people." At once they left
their nets and followed him.*

*Going on from there, he saw two other brothers, James son
of Zebedee and his brother John. They were in a boat with their
father Zebedee, preparing their nets. Jesus called them, and
immediately they left the boat and their father and followed him.*
(Matthew 4:18-22)

[Before discussing the following question during your small-group time, have group members read aloud the paragraph on pages 68–69 in *Awakening to God* that begins "Once we understand our . . ." and ends ". . . God has placed in our lives."]

2. In Matthew 4:18-22, it seems very clear that Jesus calls us to "fish for people." In what ways is that truth real in your heart, and how does it affect how you relate to people who don't know Christ?

3. When you look at the gifts God has given you and how he has used circumstances to shape you into who you are and where you are in life, how do you believe God wants to use you at this point in your life to bring the gospel to others?

Awakening to God's provision

[Before discussing the following question during your small-group time, have group members read aloud the passage on pages 82–83 in *Awakening to God* that begins "Jesus said, 'I can do nothing' . . ." and ends ". . . reach lost people through Jesus Christ."]

4. What would it look like in your day-to-day life to be intentional in sharing Christ with others while remaining totally dependent on God?

Jesus told his disciples a parable to show them that they should always pray and not give up. He said: "In a certain town there was a judge who neither feared God nor cared what people thought. And there was a widow in that town who kept coming to him with the plea, 'Grant me justice against my adversary.'

"For some time he refused. But finally he said to himself, 'Even though I don't fear God or care what people think, yet because this widow keeps bothering me, I will see that she gets justice, so that she won't eventually come and attack me!'"

And the Lord said, "Listen to what the unjust judge says. And will not God bring about justice for his chosen ones, who cry out to him day and night? Will he keep putting them off? I tell you, he will see that they get justice, and quickly. However, when the Son of Man comes, will he find faith on the earth?" (Luke 18:1-8)

5. In what ways do you want to grow in praying for those around you who don't know God?

6. What does it mean to you to "concentrate on *being* rather than doing" in fishing for people? How does *being* help in building trust?

DISCUSS

A quick note as you begin this session: These two chapters in *Awakening to God* cover a lot of ground. If necessary—and if you have flexibility within your group—you may want to take two meetings to cover this session. Take time to apply these truths in ways that will shape and transform you and others in your group to be more effective "fishers of people."

APPLY

As we seek to build genuine, trusting relationships with people who don't yet know Jesus, four practical suggestions can increase your chances of success:

- Partner with other believers.
- Look for someone who promotes peace.
- Show people the Kingdom of God.
- Keep your heart free from discouragement and disappointment.

This is where application starts to be really exciting.

In the preface to this workbook, you were encouraged to meditate on Luke 10:1-6 and to ask God to open your eyes to people around you who "promote peace." Now is the time to put this strategy into action.

A great way to incorporate some of the above elements into your daily life is to plan a service project (a day or evening when your group comes together to serve others—such as by cleaning up a struggling neighborhood, working at a food bank, or helping at a homeless shelter). Involve some of the people you've been praying for. In this way, they will experience in a practical way what the Kingdom of God in action looks like.

Another idea is to include those you're praying for and befriending in some type of affinity group at your church, whether it's playing basketball, hiking or biking together, cooking together, or some other mutually enjoyable activity that allows people to "just be" even as they're getting to know one another better.

The ideas are endless; the principle is to involve "people of peace" in working or playing together in some type of group (a "partnership of believers") where they can experience an aspect of the Kingdom of God. This way of doing something as a group also keeps people from becoming isolated and giving in to discouragement and disappointment when life gets tough.

These ideas are solid first steps that may lead you to inviting your friends to an Alpha course or some other type of relational evangelistic outreach.

FURTHER READING

Esther 4:14; Luke 12:48; Luke 19:10-27; John 17:18; John 20:21; Acts 17:26; 2 Corinthians 5:10; James 1:17; James 5:16; 1 John 5:14-15

DRAWING IN AND LANDING THE "FISH"

ENGAGE

Read chapters 8 and 9 and the epilogue in *Awakening to God: Discovering His Power and Your Purpose.*

God has called *all* Christ followers to be his witnesses (Acts 1:8) and ambassadors (2 Corinthians 5:20). To do this as God intends will require us to deny ourselves and follow Jesus (Luke 9:23). For example, when we're hurting or feel strongly about something or someone, it's not easy to keep the unity of the Spirit, to be patient, to forgive, to show kindness, or to listen to people (especially when we disagree with their views and values). And yet, this is at the core of the Christian faith and how Jesus expects us to follow him (Matthew 4:19). As we practice these principles, we will become better "fishers of people," thus showing that we love God and really are disciples of Jesus (John 14:21, 23).

Principles for introducing people to Jesus

- *Love.* Continually ask the Holy Spirit to pour God's love into your heart. "We love because he first loved us" (1 John 4:19), and his love compels us to lay down our lives for other people (2 Corinthians 5:14-15). Maintaining unity with other Christians is essential.
- *Respect.* Love others as you love yourself (Luke 10:27). Be patient, be kind, listen well, don't judge, don't backbite, be generous, show mercy and grace.
- *Ask questions.* This is the model Jesus gave us. The way to learn how to do this is to practice!
- *Learn to hear and obey* the nudges of the Holy Spirit, who lives within you.

> *Lord, thank you for calling me to know you and to participate in your great rescue mission for my family, friends, neighbors, and colleagues. Thank you for pouring your love into my heart by the Holy Spirit. Help me now to lay down my life to please you by seeking and saving those who are spiritually sinking. Amen.*

PREPARE

Drawing in the "fish"

[Before discussing the following question during your small-group time, have group members read aloud the passage on pages 105–106 in *Awakening to God* that begins "If we really love people . . ." and ends ". . . who don't yet know Christ."]

1. By now, your group is getting to know each other in a deeper and more relational way. Review chapter 8 in *Awakening to God* and reflect on the list below (which corresponds to the subheadings in the chapter). List some examples of times when you have modeled God's love in these ways. Which items on the list are areas of growth or challenge for you? Be prepared to share your examples with the group.

   - Love one another
   - Be patient
   - Demonstrate kindness
   - Respect people by how you listen
   - Do not judge
   - Show mercy and grace
   - Forgive
   - Be extravagantly generous
   - Use the special gifts that God has placed in your hands
   - Highlight the values of the Kingdom of God (affirming the ways our friends model Christ)
   - Demonstrate that your life is in Christ and not in your possessions

How to land the "fish"

2. Have you ever had the opportunity to pray with someone to surrender to Jesus Christ? Describe what happened and how it felt to be used by God in such a way.

[Before discussing the following question during your small-group time, have group members read aloud the passage on page 120 in *Awakening to God* that begins "In the Gospels, Jesus . . ." and ends ". . . come to faith in Christ."]

3. Why is asking questions—rather than having all our facts lined up or making declarative statements— often a better way to encourage people to consider the person of Jesus? What is the role of listening (both to the other person and to the Holy Spirit) in becoming "fishers of people"?

4. Jesus gave us many examples of how to communicate
   with people. Using the principles outlined below,
   how can we identify people who are "on the verge"
   of faith? Which of the following approaches have
   you used with other people, and which ones are areas
   of growth or challenge for you?

   - Jesus cared about people and treated them with
     compassion.[11]
   - Jesus gave people his full attention and wasn't
     distracted.[12]
   - Jesus asked questions.[13]
   - Jesus found a point of connection with other
     people.[14]
   - Jesus was bold and shared what he heard from
     his Father.[15]

DISCUSS

Before you discuss the questions in this section, take some time for members of the group to share about the people God used to draw them to himself, and the events leading up to their coming to Christ. Who connected with you? What were you aware of and what were you feeling at the time?

APPLY

As we come down the homestretch of our study of *Awakening to God*, we hope and believe that God is changing you and everyone in your group.

Here are some ways to help facilitate that change:

- Break into smaller groups of two or three people, and take some time to role-play one of the following:

  - Sharing a simple gospel message—explaining the gospel to the other person as simply as you can

- Leading someone in a prayer of salvation

- Inviting someone to church, an Alpha course, or another evangelistic initiative

- If you haven't yet done so, invite someone to the service project or "affinity group" that your group has planned or is involved in.

- Take some time to pray in groups of two or three for those whom you're continuing to love and reach out to.

The epilogue may be difficult for some people to read, just as it was difficult for Gerard to write it. Still, it is important that we grapple with the challenge Gerard presents—not to stand by and watch people sink spiritually without trying to rescue them. In your smaller group of two or three, discuss your responses to the epilogue and how God is speaking to your heart at this time.

As a Christ follower, what are the changes you're making—by God's grace—to become a man or woman authentically engaged in fishing for people?

FURTHER READING

Matthew 5:16; Matthew 7:1-2; Matthew 9:36-38; Matthew 22:39; Luke 6:36-38; Luke 19:1-10; John 1:12; John 5:24; John 17:20-23; 2 Timothy 4:1-2; James 1:19-20

Notes

1. Acts 17:6, NKJV
2. Matthew 4:19
3. Ibid.
4. John 8:31-32
5. James 2:14-17
6. John 16:13
7. Matthew 16:15
8. John 14:21, 23; John 17:4; Ephesians 2:10
9. Colossians 2:6-7, NLT
10. Gerard Long, *Awakening to God* (Carol Stream, IL: Tyndale House Publishers, 2014), 17.
11. Matthew 9:36; Matthew 14:14; Matthew 15:32; Matthew 20:34
12. Mark 10:46-52
13. Luke 5:23; Luke 6:39-42; Luke 8:25
14. John 4:7-26, 39-42; John 11:28-44
15. John 5:30; John 8:28, 42; John 12:49

About the Authors

GERARD LONG is a minister, evangelist, author, motivational speaker, and former banking executive. He is currently the executive director of Alpha USA, a nonprofit organization that introduces people to Christianity through courses supported by multidenominational churches in more than 169 countries. More than three million people have taken an Alpha course in the United States and more than twenty-four million worldwide.

BRUCE FARLEY is the regional director for northeast Ohio Alpha USA. His goal is to increase the number and effectiveness of Alpha courses in northeast Ohio so that thousands might come into a life-changing, authentic, and growing relationship with Jesus Christ. Over the past twenty-five years, Bruce has served in a variety of pastoral roles, most recently as pastor of spiritual formation for Journey Community Church in Fairview Park, Ohio, and as lead pastor of RiverChurch in Olmsted Falls, Ohio.

Where are my keys

Am I at the right job

Is there more to life than this

Alpha

Everyone has questions

Alpha is a series of interactive sessions that freely explore the basics of the Christian faith in a friendly, honest and informal environment. **No pressure. No follow up. No charge.**

Start an Alpha near you. alphausa.org #RunAlpha

To complete this workbook, get your copy of *Awakening to God* today, and fulfill God's calling in your life.

Foreword by BILL HYBELS

AWAKENING TO GOD

Discovering his power and your purpose

GERARD LONG
Executive Director of Alpha USA